SourdoughBaker's

Sourdough Fermentation Mini Guide

A short guide to basic sourdough fermentation principles for the home baker.

By Warwick Quinton

Warwick Quinton is one of Australia's original artisan bakers. He has been plying his trade for almost three decades, and is considered a world expert on practical sourdough bread making.

His 'Sourdough 101' technique is both simple and profound. This mini guide is intended as a starting point towards understanding authentic sourdough fermentation.

In this series of Mini Guides, a complete and detailed picture of the entire sourdough process is built up, from Prefermentation to Baking with Thermal Mass.

Warwick's skill at providing accurate, detailed and practical advice to home bakers is well known. He has been teaching his popular Sourdough 101 Series of workshops for the past ten years.

His website and blog has become a 'go to' site for serious bakers, as it is more than authoritative; its information has been gathered from hard won experience.

In recent years he has become obsessed with wood fired ovens, and now designs and consults around low tech bakery set ups. His ovens are both practical, long lasting and capable of baking bread to the highest standard possible.

Keep an eye on sourdoughbaker.com.au or Amazon.com.au for additions to this range of mini guides.

Warwick teaches his craft to home bakers and the trade from his 'Bush Bakery' in the lower Hunter Valley of NSW.

Contents:

Introduction

Sourdough Fermentation Mini Guide

Sourdough Bread is the original bread. It has been created as a staple part of many diets for centuries. Bread is, by nature, a fermented product – and when we make it, we are learning to manage a natural fermentation process.

The texture and the flavour of real sourdough bread can be attributed to this process deliberately being kept as slow as possible. The slow fermentation creates gases inside the dough, as the carbohydrate in the dough begins to ferment. These gases are trapped in stretchy folds of gluten and vegetable gum, which are gently drawn out of the natural grain through the process of dough making. The baker then 'rounds' each piece of slowly fermenting dough to help to capture this gas in bubbles.

As the gas given off by the fermentation process expands, the baker's dough becomes light. Good bakers will 'round' their dough more than once, so that the structure of the bubbles is strengthened.

Finally, when the dough is perfectly ripe, it is shaped, scored and baked.

There is so much more to a good loaf of bread than meets the senses. But even the bit that meets the senses is pretty amazing.

Welcome to the world of real sourdough breadmaking!

Mass production equals waste

All breads made today are offshoots of various sourdough methods. Unfortunately, due to our century old obsession with efficiency, natural fermentation has all but disappeared from the bread making process.

We have made so much bread the western world is overfull and obese. And not just bread. All staple products are over supplied – and the result is, ultimately, a chubby population.

Much of this bread, as well as other staples, is made to fill shelves in retail outlets. Nature abhors a vacuum, apparently. This 'shelf filler' will never be sold, and in most cases, humans won't be eating it – at least not directly. When a bakery is on the city fringe, livestock owners take it away by the bin full and use it to fatten their pigs or cattle. A tiny amount of all this wasted bread sometimes goes to homeless people, though there is far more waste than homeless people can possibly eat.

Recently, there have been moves both in Australia and overseas to provide this waste bread for sale at special 'food thrift' outlets, which sell blemished, out of date or wasted food.

Despite all of these things, the largest amount of waste bread just disappears into landfill.

We don't need more bread. We need to knead more bread.

The Antidote

When you bake sourdough yourself, you learn as you bake, making it a deeply efficient activity.

As a bonus, you discover how nutritious and digestible slowly leavened bread is. You simply won't be able to eat mass produced bread ever again!

After baking just a few proper sourdough loaves, you begin to understand lots of things in a different way.

Those who persevere with natural baking gain a good solid working knowledge of many things, including fermentation, the effects of heat and cold, what ripeness actually is, flour quality, water quality, the seasons; and so much more.

When you bake using a true sourdough culture, with flour,

> The semi constant and very satisfying process of making bread at home, in your own kitchen, nourishes you, your family and your friends directly. It also nourishes your mind, and all your senses, in a way that not many other things can.

water and salt only, these things gradually reveal themselves to you. When you are getting started, there are many online information resources, like sourdoughbaker.com.au, to help you get your head around it all.

Nature can easily become subjugated to the chemical world when we add things like commercial yeast and bread improver to flour and water. The only thing we learn when we use these chemicals is 'how to do', rather than 'why to do'.

The longer and more often you bake, the more you understand what an amazing thing bread is; how primal it is to us and our civilisation. Once you think you have it all figured out, along comes something unexpected, and you once again become mystified. The natural processes involved in the fermentation and baking of bread are so different to those in our pushbutton, digitized world. By engaging with these natural processes with an open and curious mind, we stay mentally healthy. Nutrition is not just about the gut – it's about the mind as well. You still can't push a button to recreate what you learn to make with two hands and a mind.

Great bakers think 'organically'. There is no short cut available. Experience is the only true teacher.

When you begin to get the gist of it all, the processes become part of your own rhythm, and organic thinking gradually subverts the digitized 'how to' world.

When you tend to your starter; when you create a pre ferment; when you knead dough by hand or in a mixer, when you ripen dough properly, and then work that dough with your hands; when you finally shape and dust and score the ripened dough; when your bread 'kicks' in the oven; when you get to experience all that transformation in every mouthful of beautifully baked sourdough bread. That's when you start to experience 'organic thinking'.

As a bonus, your homemade bread almost always tastes great – even your 'less than best' efforts. Well-made bread also keeps far better than commercially made bread.

You will find that when bread becomes a precious resource, very little is wasted.

Let's Start at the Starter

You are about to become the proud creator / owner of a 'desem', or 'dough starter'.

A dough starter is a proper starter. It's all grown up.

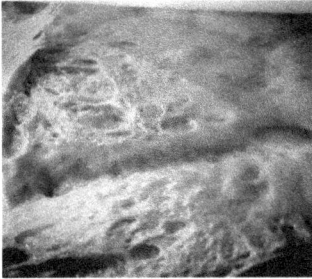

It's not fickle and attention seeking, like liquid starters are. It doesn't ask for complicated modifications to recipes and for total adherence to one recipe only, like 'old dough' starters do.

Dough starters are stable beasts, and yet powerful. They have a different mix of enzymes in them to the more commonly found liquid starters. Thus, they behave quite differently in dough. Their relatively stable structure becomes a template for the final 'crumb' in the bread – so the loose, open texture you love in good sourdough begins here.

Dough starters, when coupled with an old fashioned baker's technique known as 'prefermentation', can create a taste in the finished bread that is more pronounced, deeper and more 'sour.'

A more accurate description of the unique taste we find in properly made sourdough bread might be found in the Japanese word '*umami*' – which can be loosely defined as the flavour of fermentation.

According to Japanese thought, umami is one of the five fundamental taste sensations.

There are many other types of 'starter'. Many cultures use short term yeasted starters like the *biga* or the *poolish*. Throughout Europe you will find sweetened starters like 'honey salt'. There are mash starters, linking bakeries and breweries since the beginnings of village life. There are potato starters, and other pure starch starters which have been utilised throughout industry as well as in kitchens around the world. There are yogurt and curd starters, as well as starters cultured from mushrooms, grapes and other fruits as well as vegetables.

Liquid vs Dough Starters

Liquid Starter

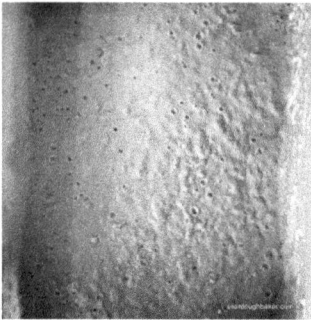

You will no doubt have seen tubs of liquid starter bubbling away on YouTube, or as pictures in sourdough blogs and recipe books. Liquid starters are generally classified by their consistency being roughly one part water to one part flour. They are where every budding sourdough baker begins their sourdough journey.

I prefer to classify them as 'pourable' starters. Different feeding regimes exist, and so flour and water ratios vary a bit, but generally this 'one to one' ratio is within the ball park of what is used.

A method commonly found in artisan bakeries in the USA involves many feeds of the starter each day, with constant monitoring required. They make their starter a little more 'runny', so that it ferments quickly. By doing this, they maintain the types of enzymes needed to produce a consistent flavour and texture in their bread.

My own bakery in the Blue Mountains needed to maintain a base of about 150kg of liquid starter, which would be fed each day. It was kept at a typical one to one flour to water ratio, and ripened within six hours, even in the coolroom. Indeed, the rather large tub of sourdough starter rarely left the coolroom at all.

The big problem with liquid starters is also their strong point; they ripen quite rapidly. This means they become over ripe quickly too. Knowing when to feed any starter takes a bit of experience, but when you are using a liquid starter, the issue is amplified. I see beginners over feeding their starter all too often. When they do this, it takes a while to fully manifest as a problem – but when it does, it can be quite difficult to undo.

Conversely, people forget to feed them, and return to find their precious sourdough starter has become pretty low grade hooch. Once this occurs, the starter will take quite a lot of work to bring back to a workable state.

Thus, I call liquid starters 'fickle'. They change with the hour. They are not as powerful as dough starters either. As a result, they take up more room in the fridge, because you need more of them to do the job of making dough rise..

Dough Starter:

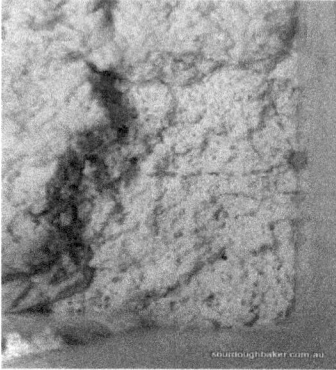

Dough starters could generally be regarded as having a ratio of two parts flour to one part water. At this consistency, the starter can't be poured.

Dough starters, for my money, are where it's at. They are amazingly stable – I once made a YouTube clip which shows me repairing a starter which hadn't been fed for over a year – and in the clip, it shows what good shape the 'core' starter was in, despite being almost completely consumed by fungus around the outside.

The interesting thing about them is their strength. I use about the same percentage of dough starter as I would use fresh yeast in a recipe – about one percent – and still get amazing flavour and a good rise.

Monitoring the ripeness of a dough starter is quite easy, and indeed whether it is perfectly ripe or not won't make a huge difference to the finished bread, particularly if you are using pre fermentation.

I acknowledge reality though. Dough starters do better when prefermentation in the bread making process is used, and this is sometimes inconvenient. However, you only need to keep a preferment for a day at a time. By comparison, a liquid starter needs attention almost every day!

In the scheme of things, liquid starters represent a risk, as well as more work for the home baker than the easy to maintain dough starter.

How much starter should I use?

If you use prefermentation, dough starter can be as little as 1% of dough weight. I use this percentage in my really slow fermented doughs. It's easy to weigh out 200 grams of starter for a 20 kg dough. (Note: More on the subject of slow fermentation in an upcoming Mini Guide 'The really Slow Sourdough Fermentation Guide'.)

In small doughs, say up to a couple of kilos, 2% to 3% will do nicely – assuming you will be using an overnight pre ferment. You see, because starter is a living thing, the amount you use simply changes the rate of fermentation. With a small dough, such as the one you will be making in the recipe following later, I have found this percentage is easier to work with.

For faster fermentation, use up to 10% of dough weight. Warning: things speed up quite a lot, so really slow fermentation (72 hours or more) isn't possible. At levels of ten percent, the dough will break down quite quickly, even if it is kept cold.

As you can see, dough starter very flexible to use. Essentially, the longer you wish to ferment your dough, the less dough starter you use. The opposite can also be true. A fast dough needs more starter – especially if you ARE NOT using prefermentation.

One does have to be mindful of temperature control throughout these processes. In a nutshell: lower temperature equals slower fermentation. Slower fermentation means deeper, more complex flavours in the bread you bake. Really slow fermentation (up to 90 hours from start to finish) means a slightly more dense bread, with incredible keeping qualities and even more flavour.

Fast fermentation equates to a milder flavour, shorter keeping qualities, and a slightly bigger rise.

What's prefermentation?

The recipe later on in this booklet relies on prefermentation. This technique is used by many artisan bakers around the world, and has variants like the Italian '*biga*'; the French '*poolish*'; and the Australian '*sponge*'. These examples are all made using regular refined yeast. Bakers know that by using prefermentation they will get better crust and more open crumb in their bread. If you spend time working with master bakers, you will find they tend to incorporate some type of prefermentation in almost all their recipes. In a sense, prefermentation makes sourdough starter more potent. It's a very useful thing to understand.

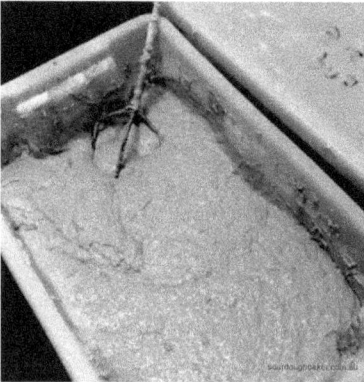

For many years, I placed prefermentation into one of those 'interesting but fiddly' activities bakers do – and from working in a bakery with a variety of trade bakers over the years, there are plenty of things which easily fall into this category. Not everything bakers do is absolutely necessary, so at that time I edited this activity from the routine.

However, after having quietly played around with it for the past eight years, I can tell you that when using a dough starter, prefermentation is definitely my preferred option – at least for the type of fermentation I do – which is extremely slow (by comparison with other bakers). My standard practice ends up being about 72 hours from starter to oven. There will be more on this in my 'Really Slow Fermentation Guides. Keep an eye out for it.

Even when used in conjunction with a liquid starter, prefermentation improves the crust and crumb of every loaf of bread. Indeed, the French, Italian, Swiss and German bakers I've worked with over the years all used different versions in their own traditional bread making practices.

There are quite a lot of little techniques that bakers employ to both save them work and to make better bread. I guess I've sponged a few of these myself – and it never ceases to amaze me that proper bakers are considered 'semi-skilled'!

The first part of the recipe following, where you add the starter, water and half the flour, is how we get things going using a very small amount of starter.

A complete, simple recipe system using desem, or dough starter, is in my Sourdough 101 and 102 Workshop Notes, which are available to download on the website, www.sourdoughbaker.com.au.

After having made artisan breads in all sorts of ways for a few decades now, the way I make bread has evolved to a core method, based around the use of this desem, coupled with the other essential ingredient, prefermentation. Once these two are in place, the baker can make extraordinary sourdough breads.

'The natural fermentation of dough is returning to the center of the baker's craft. It's a worldwide phenomenon, and it has risen up because as humans, our connection to real bread is deeper and more primal than anyone ever imagined. In many ways, bread is representative of our entire progress as a species; where we have come from, where we are, and where we could be'.

Basic Sourdough Recipe

This recipe makes enough dough for two 750g loaves.

Step 1: Mix Preferment

Place up to 50 mils of dough starter in 500 mils of water.

Allow to stand for up to 30 minutes to soften. Add 500 grams of flour, and whisk everything together and seal the container.

Step 2: Ripen it

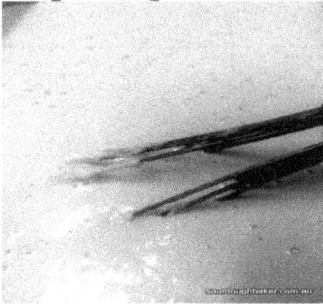

Leave to stand overnight in cooler weather, or for a whole day in the fridge. The preferment should now be filled with bubbles. If not, don't worry. Your bread will still work. If you really want, you can leave it for another day in the fridge.

Step 3: Autolyse ('shaggy dough')

Mix in another 500 grams of flour.

Don't worry if the dough is all shaggy and messy – just try to get all the flour into it. Allow to stand for up to 2 hours. This is known as 'shaggy dough', or the 'autolyse'.

Step 4: Salt and Kneading

Add up to 20 grams of salt, and give the whole thing a good kneading. The more you knead the dough, the better your bread will be.

Kneading can be done more effectively by incorporating some 20 minute 'rests' into the routine – dough develops more easily after a short rest. When finished, you have enough dough for two loaves of bread.

Step 5: First (Bulk) Proof

Allow dough to rise for approximately 4 hours. It should double in size by this time. Alternately, you can pop it in the fridge overnight. In cooler weather, things slow down – as is the case when you put the dough in the fridge to ripen.

Sourdough is tied to the weather, so times can vary quite a bit.

Rule of thumb: wait for the dough to double in size before proceeding to the next step.

Step 6: Second (Cut) proof

Remove the dough from the container and divide it in two. Shape the two chunks into balls, with a smooth surface exposed and the seam at the bottom. Place back into the sealed container. Allow to rise again for 2 more hours. Again, the dough should double in size. In cooler weather, this can take longer. In hot weather, things will go faster.

In the picture, you can see many more balls of dough starting their second proof. This is exactly how we do it in the bakery – so instead of two balls of dough, we make many!

Step 7: Third (Final) proof

Mould the balls of dough into cylinders. Cover a wooden board in coarse semolina or good quality baking paper. Place the cylinders onto the board. Dust with more semolina, score, and allow to soften (say, another hour).

Step 8: Bake

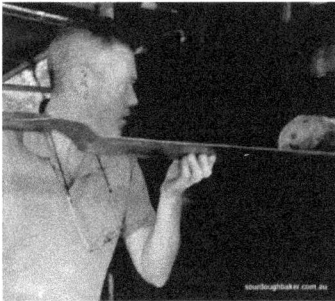

Slide the shaped, scored and proofed cylinders onto a hot baking stone in your oven. Bake for approximately 30 – 45 minutes at 220 C. It's a good idea to turn the breads in their place, end to end, after about fifteen minutes. Once again, if your oven is right, your dough will double the size.

And there, in our hands, we have a finished loaf of true sourdough bread!

Keep an eye out for an upcoming guide, which will be called "The Really Good Guide to Bread Ovens".

Feeding and maintaining your Dough Starter

Dough starter's consistency is **two parts flour to one part water**.

In these notes, grams will equal milliliters – so a gram of flour equals a millilitre of water. For such small volumes, weighing water is unnecessary.

With dough starter, it's a good idea to keep four times to eight times the amount of starter you're going to need in any one dough. That way, you only need to feed it every four bakes, which saves time and effort. For example, when I'm baking at home, I like to keep about 400 grams of starter as my 'full' amount, so that I've still got 200 grams left after a few uses.

Usually, when I'm just baking a few loaves, I might only use 50 grams of starter each time – so I'll get about four uses before I need to feed my starter.

Sometimes, people put two lines around their jar of starter – one to indicate its volume when it's just been fed (i.e., when it's full), and the other about half way down to the bottom from this full point (i.e., when it needs to be fed). So when the starter gets down to that bottom line, they feed it. If you do this, remember to leave about the same amount of airspace above the top line as the volume of the starter when it's just been fed. That way, there will always be enough air for the starter to breathe.

Feeding example:

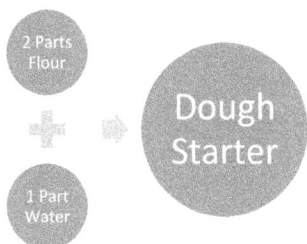

Okay, so let's say, via whatever means, we have ended up at your bottom line on the starter jar. When the jar is at its top line, it contains about 400 grams of starter. We've used about half so far. For the sake of simplicity, let's say we are feeding to replace 210 grams used (about half). This equates to three parts of 70 grams or mils each. Nice round numbers. Bakers like round numbers.

First, you will need 70 mls of water. Add that to the remaining starter, and allow the water to soak into it. You can help it along with a fork, potato masher or whisk.

Note: Measurements are not critical here.
Let ratios be your guiding principle.
Remember, *2 parts flour to one part water.*

Next, add 140 grams of flour to the hydrated starter. Work the hydrated mixture and the flour together. You should be able to make the dough starter take up all the flour, so that the sides of your container are free from flour.

Viola! Your starter is fed. Now, simply return your desem to the fridge and allow it to ripen.

When you double the volume of your remaining starter after a feed, as we have done here, ripeness will be achieved after a day in the fridge, or overnight if you leave it out.

Starter storage

Starter is a living thing. In general, a dough starter is best kept in low temperatures.

Bacteriological and yeasting activities vary according to temperature. If these microbiomes are accustomed to cold temperature then they are best kept in the cold. Having flemish roots, the technique of keeping a desem (which we've been calling a 'dough starter') could be said to be a native of the cold. At fridge temperatures, a desem is very stable, and stays ripe for a long time. If you leave it out of the fridge, it will ripen more quickly, but it will soon become overripe.

The default option for starter storage is, then, your refrigerator. When starter is stored below ten degrees centigrade, it will remain ripe much longer than if you leave it out.

How Ripe is my Starter?

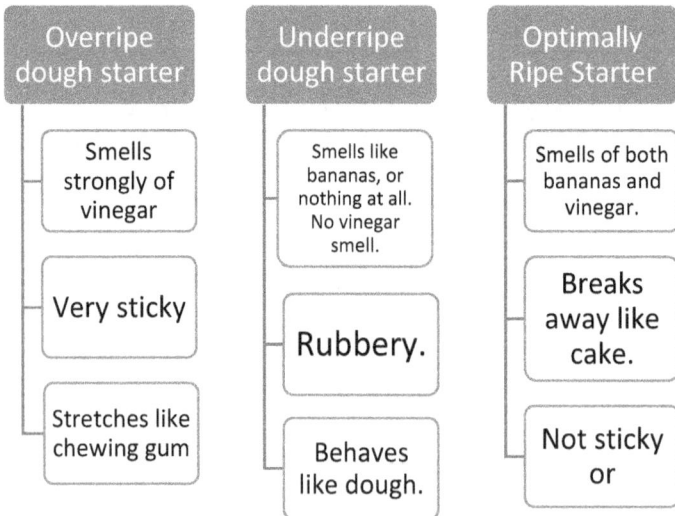

Overripe dough starter	Underripe dough starter	Optimally Ripe Starter
Smells strongly of vinegar	Smells like bananas, or nothing at all. No vinegar smell.	Smells of both bananas and vinegar.
Very sticky	Rubbery.	Breaks away like cake.
Stretches like chewing gum	Behaves like dough.	Not sticky or

You can tell when a desem is overripe. The proteins break down and the dough becomes very sticky, and then stretchy – like chewing gum. That's because after the proteins have broken down, the bacteria inside the starter eat into the remaining substance of carbohydrate and alcohol, creating a type of vegetable gum.

This overripe starter is accompanied by a strong smell of vinegar. These two telltale signs – the pungent smell of vinegar and the sticky, stretchy texture – are indications that your starter should be fed before it is next used.
An underripe starter is exactly like dough – still a bit stretchy, a bit rubbery, but not sticky. There is very little smell. You may get a faint smell of bananas – the gas which smells like bananas is called ethylene – and it is given off when fermentation begins to occur. It's a good sign to be able to smell this gas – it means there is fermentation happening.

When your starter dough is still very 'dough like', and there is very little smell, it might be best to allow the starter to ripen a bit longer before you use it. If you are in a hurry, you can ripen it out of the fridge overnight. Otherwise, it will ripen quite happily in the fridge over the next few days.

Later, the smell will change to include the smell of vinegar as well. This smell tells you that there is alcohol production – and so a complete process of fermentation is underway.

The presence of both smells, then, tells us that we are dealing with optimally ripe starter. The texture of desem that is nicely ripe could be best described as like a 'cake' – it breaks away from itself quite easily, and is not overly stretchy or 'gummy'.

Over time, you will be able to quickly assess the ripeness of your starter. While the desem starter can be used successfully whether it is under or over ripe, best results are gained when the starter is optimally ripe.

What are the best types of flour for feeding my starter?

Different flours provide different types of food for a starter.

Some people will have us believe that a starter gathers airborne yeasts to become active. While this is partly true, the vast majority of the wild yeasts in starter actually come from the grain that feeds it. The grain accumulates wild yeasts under the surface of the bran layer. That's why wholegrain flours contain more yeasts than flours where the bran has been removed. True whole grain flours are more yeasty, then, than white ones. Breads made with wholegrain starters tend towards faster fermentation, as the yeast is doing most of the work.

But yeast is only half the story. Your starter does its thing (convert carbohydrates to simple sugars) also via bacteria – which once again is both air and grain borne. In addition, your starter gets its bacteria from our skin, which is abundant with a type of bacteria called *lactobacillus sanfranciscensis*. This bacteria is key in producing lactic acid, a fundamental part of the sourdough flavour we have all come to know and love.

Feeding a starter with white or heavily sifted flour will reduce the 'yeastiness' of the starter, and in so doing, promote the work of bacteria. Essentially, a starter culture arrives at kind of consensus amongst the beasties therein to work towards a common aim – so if the yeasts don't break down the carbohydrates, then the bacteria will do it – but in their way, rather than the way the yeast does it. So a 'white' starter can be said to produce 'tangier' bread, as there are more lactic acids given off by the dominant bacteriological processes going on. However, there are other ways to produce 'tanginess' in bread – and the type of starter used really is just a small part of it.

Of course, bacteria don't live in isolated colonies, and there are hundreds if not thousands of different types of bacteria involved in the sourdough process.

How do I prepare my starter for a long period without a feed?

This question is possibly the most common one I've heard in regards to sourdough starter. How do we put starter into hibernation?

People become quite attached to their starters, and often name them. They certainly don't want them to die while they are on holidays.
The good news is, it's quite easy to prepare a starter for a long snooze. Here are a few quick scenarios:

1/. Q: I'm going away for a couple days. Do I need to worry about my starter?

A: No.

2/. Q: I'm going away for a couple of weeks. Do I need to worry about my starter?

A: Probably not. Your starter, if regularly fed and maintained, will be fine for a two week snooze. If you feel that it is already a bit overripe, try covering it in flour and pushing this flour into it before you go. The starter should look like a reasonably tough ball of dough. Leave it in the fridge as usual.

3/. Q: I'm going away for a couple of months. How should I prepare my starter?

A: About a week before you go, do the same as for the previous question. Then, a few days later, repeat the process – you may need to add just a drizzle of water to help the flour to combine. Then, just before you go, repeat the process again. You will now have a very tough and dense ball of dough. This consistency of starter dough can be kept for up to six months without feeding at all, and can usually be brought back to active with a minimum of fuss when you return.

4/. Q: I'm going away for a year or so, and I'm going to turn off the fridge. How can I keep my starter?

A: Simply make the starter into a ball, coat it in flour, and place it in the middle of a bag of flour. Seal the bag, and put it in a cool, dry place. Over time, the starter will dry out and become almost like a stone. However, the flour provides the starter with everything it needs to survive.

When you get back, take the starter out of the flour, place it into a mortar and pestle, and break open the ball of starter. Have a look at what you have. If there is a layer of a green mould in the inside of the ball when you crack it open, scrape this out with a spoon. It's not, despite appearances, all that bad – what you are doing here is removing the dead crust of the mould around your starter.

What's left, after you have scraped the green stuff off, is workable to reconstitute – even if there is a smidgeon of mould left on it. Grind the remainder up into a coarse flour consistency, and rehydrate with enough water to cover the powder. You can mash it up a bit in the water to help it along. Leave it with the water overnight – just cover it so it doesn't crust up or become contaminated. Next day, add a little flour to bring it back to a dough consistency. Give it a bit of a knead – not a lot, just enough to get all the flour and liquid combined. It will be ready to use in about twelve hours' time.

Dough Starter is, as I have said many times before, as close to immortal as it gets.

What's this mould growing all over my starter?

From time to time you may observe varying amounts of mould growing on the surface of the desem. Both yeast and mould are different types of fungus, and as such there are similarities. Mould tends to grow in damp places – so if you have a sealed lid on your starter container, condensation from the refrigeration can begin to form mould on top of your starter dough.

The issue isn't really resolved by removing the lid either – now the mould can crust up due to exposure to the air. It's also possible that other moulds, dormant in your fridge, can now reproduce. Thus, the old idea of keeping a starter out and covered in muslin may well be okay in Europe, but in Australia will lead to issues.

Happily, though, the solution to this conundrum is straightforward. When a mould, whether light or heavy, forms on your dough starter, simply cut it off. The mould will be very happy to live in your compost. After a year or three, the mould will suck the life out of your starter if you leave it where it is. Don't worry, you have as much as a few years before this is likely to occur.

Fundamentally, the layer of mould which is covering the starter is actually, in the short to medium term, protecting it from harm. It does this by covering the surface of the dough starter with itself. The mould extracts nutrients from the starter in tiny amounts – but in the main, also protects the dough starter from moisture loss and attack by other yeasts and moulds. It's a kind of symbiotic relationship – there is excess water in the environment, and the mould is happy to consume it.

Over time, and without a sufficiently large 'bed' of starter, this mould will take hold of the starter and literally consume it.

I have rescued starters at all stages of mould consumption. I have had to remove up to nine tenths of the starter – but inside all the mould is almost always a tiny chunk of beautifully preserved *desem* – and the similarities between it and fresh yeast visually are quite startling. Feeding up this tiny fresh and clean starter after removing a lot of mould is quite easy.

I simply double its volume (by weighing it), and wait for it to ripen (usually out of the fridge). Once it is ripe, I'll double it again. If it is a really big starter, or if I started from a tiny chunk, I might double it again after a similar ripening period. The mathematics are simple and beautiful – and, by only doubling the 'bed' each time, the starter recovers and grows very quickly.

Once the starter is close to a size that is workable, I simply pop it in the fridge and leave it until ripened for use – which will be very quickly, because after a couple of feeds in quick succession, the micro greeblies are feeling fit and frisky.

When you work with fermentation, a little mould is a part of life. Moulds and yeasts are both fungi, but of different types. When a sourdough starter is regularly fed, and ideally, kept in a cool, dry environment, moulds will be invisible – they are there, almost certainly, but dormant; they can perceive when there is excess moisture, and at this time, they will begin replicating. As such, most of the time, the mould is almost imperceptible. I don't go to any great trouble to clean it off. If it builds up, I remove it like a kind of crust, and the remaining starter beneath will be sweet and delicious.

I work with the same 'line on the jar' principle I mentioned earlier – only on a larger scale. When my container is close to the bottom, I mix the remaining starter with 3 litres of water and 6 kg of flour. Even if there is only a kilogram of the starter remaining before the feed, the starter is ready for action after one night left out of the fridge (or about four days if left in the fridge to ripen).

My dough starter usually fluctuates between about a kilo (low, low mark) and twelve kilos (really, really full). It tends to re ripen after any sized feed really quickly. If you have this booklet as a result of purchasing the same starter, I believe you can rest assured this old beasty is tough enough for anything you can dish out.

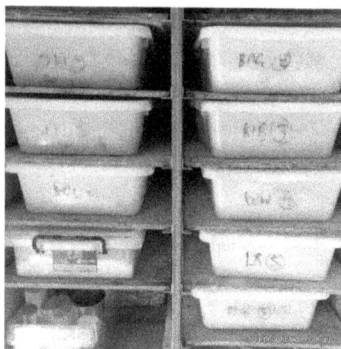

At times, when I am doing a lot of production work, feeding occurs about once a week. There are also times when I'm not doing production work, and my starter frequently goes for two or three weeks between feeds. At these times, I might need to remove a bit of mould from the top of my starter when I come to feed it after a big break. Wastage in these cases is usually minimal, though, as the amount removed is perhaps 1% of the total or even less.

At home, you will be working with significantly smaller volumes. The key thing is to maintain the ratio of 2 parts flour to one part water. This way, your starter is thick enough to have some shelf life, yet there is enough liquid there to fully soak all the flour.

What are 'proofs'?

Bread is, by definition, baked gluten bubbles. As dough ferments, it develops gas inside its gluten network. This gas, carbon dioxide, must be expelled from time to time so that the gluten network can transform from a web like structure to sheets of gluten, and finally bubbles. By expelling this carbon dioxide, we are mechanically assisting the sticky gluten network to join together strands, and as gas forms, these strands are stretched into sheets. Further removal of gas seals these sheets up in places, creating bubbles.

> *The proofing process is the generation of gas via fermentation, and then the removal of this gas via mechanical means. Each time the gas is generated and then removed is called a 'proof'.*

The Proofing Process

In the recipe earlier, we could say there are three 'proofs'. **The first proof**, which at room temperature would be about 4 hours long according to the recipe, is known in the trade as the 'bulk' or 'primary' proof. The first proof continues and accelerates the fermentation which began by the pre fermentation process we spoke about earlier. The completed dough, containing all the flour, all the water and the salt, can now spend four hours out of the fridge. In this time, it simply produces CO_2 gas as it ferments, safe in the knowledge that the well-made dough will capture this gas. Over time, the captured gas will help the gluten network to mash together and then to stretch into thin, single celled frames. Very little Co_2 will be lost during this proof, and so big gluten bubbles will be made by the end of this proof.

The gas eventually causes the whole fermentation process to slow down, as it has nowhere to go. When it is evacuated, the next proof begins.

The second proof in the recipe is only half as long – 2 hours – and this proof is known in the trade as the 'middle' or 'intermediate' proof. It occurs after the bulk proof has been completed; in other words, the maximum level of gas has been produced from the first fermentation, and is then removed - usually by the dough being cut up into two (or more) pieces and 'rough rounded'. The rough rounding process creates a skin around the fermenting ball of dough, which is necessary to contain the next stage of fermentation. By containing the gas, then expelling it repeatedly, we are strengthening the gluten network.

In recipe books, this process is also referred to as 'pre shaping' or 'punching down' – though in our technique, punching down is not really what we are doing. Nonetheless, the object of the second proof is to remove gas while at the same time creating a perfect environment for more gas to be captured as the fermentation process begins again.

The second proof condenses the gluten network, allowing for the loose structure to be stretched and folded in on itself. This means there will be more, slightly smaller bubbles, and the cell walls of each bubbles will become progressively thinner. This second proof actually creates the necessary strength in the dough structure to be able to stand up on its own in the oven, rather than relying on the walls of a bread tin.

The third and final proof does the same thing as the other two proofs, and it also sets the shape of the finished bread. It allows maximum volume in the baked loaf if done correctly – and also for there to be a successful oven 'spring'.

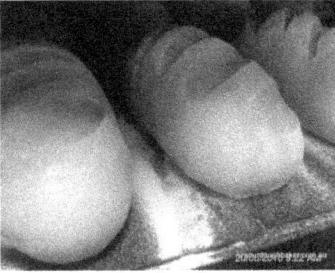

By the time the final proof is ready to begin, the fermentation process is fully underway. That's why the third proof is only half as long again – an hour at room temperature, approximately. By the time the dough has had its gas removed two times already, the gluten walls are now very thin. This means that the bread will be light, but it also means that the dough is now becoming a bit delicate to handle. It's important to do as little as possible in this final shaping. It's really a matter of simply turning out your ripened balls of dough onto the bench, gently separating them (if there is more than one piece of dough) and folding under the sides (if you are making a cylindrical shaped bread).

Why three proofs?

In recipe books, you will often see there are often only two proofs required. This is the case when using a bread tin or a banneton – when you do this, you can pretty much skip the middle proof, because the tin will support the dough as it rises.

By adding an extended middle proof, you are effectively conditioning the dough to stand proud, without the need for something to hold it up. The recipe that came with the starter has three proofs because it was designed as a recipe for 'sole baked' bread – bread that is baked directly on the sole of the oven. Refer to the Sourdough 101 notes for more information on this process.

From my years in bakeries, I'll add a trade secret for you:

Bakers always allow some time for an intermediate proof – even if they are using tins. The middle proof strengthens the gluten network, and so when the bread is baked, it stands up taller and more 'integral' to itself. The bread, when three proofs have been done, looks like it wants to climb right out of the tin.

Indeed, when you are sole baking, instead of using a tin, you will find that this middle proof is the most important of all!

Checking for ripeness

Dough can be quite easily assessed for its state of ripeness, whether it is in the first, second or third proof.

It's important to understand by touch and by sight as to when a dough is ready to be moved from one stage of proofing to the next.

The finished bread has better shape, is larger, and has substantially improved keeping qualities if the dough has been allowed to ripen and be de gassed at the optimal times throughout the entire proofing process.

Bakers become adept at making judgement calls. When you start out, this is daunting, and some new bakers struggle knowing when a dough is ripe. There is a bit of trial and error involved; however, for the creation of a beautifully shaped loaf of bread which colours to bright orange or caramel in the oven, you need to understand ripeness.

Judgement calls?

A judgement call is made by assessing and then weighing up a number of criteria. I use a point scoring system. In terms of ripeness, my criteria are:

> *To understand ripeness, you need to learn how to make judgement calls.*

1/. **Volume:** Has the dough doubled in size since the beginning of the stage?

2/. **Wobble factor**: Does the dough wobble in, or on, its container? When you shake the container it's in, how much wobble is there?

3/. **Poke test**: If I poke the dough with my finger, how does it bounce back? If it's rubbery and bounces back quickly, it will fail the poke test. If it's soft, like ripe brie cheese, and bounces back very slowly, then it passes the poke test.

Each of these three criteria can be scored with either a zero (not at all), a one (somewhat), or a two (definitely).
Thus, a perfect score would be six points – meaning that all three criteria have been 'definitely' satisfied. This translates to yes, it has definitely doubled in volume, yes, it wobbles a lot, and yes, it is soft and doesn't bounce back when I poke it.

Compromises

In a bakery situation, where time is critical, I would be satisfied with a score of four out of six. At home, it's easier to go for five or six – though time can also play a part here, so my advice is to simply say that it's rarely a perfect world.

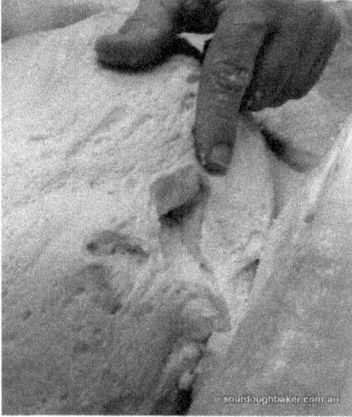

Though a score of three using this process may result in edible bread, there's a pretty fair chance you could be headed for disappointment.

Disappointment isn't good for the mental space. We all know that. Why risk it?

While I can point out the main criteria for each of these things, in the end only practical, hands on experience counts. I strongly recommend that the best way to understand this stuff is to do it for yourself.

Of course, if you haven't already attended a Sourdough 101 Workshop at our Bush Bakery in the Hunter Valley of NSW, and you can find the time, I'll shamelessly promote this as a really good way to get further into home sourdough breadmaking than you ever thought possible. I cover all the information here, and much more besides.

Learning to make sourdough bread is, in the main, a solitary pursuit. It can be really frustrating at first when things don't work out well; equally, there are always new challenges which force you out of your comfort zone.

Working in a class setup can get you a lot further down the track more quickly than all the online or written resources in the world. In addition, making bread is a very tactile thing. It really helps to see, feel and taste things. It also helps to get together with a bunch of others who are all at different stages of learning, as they will almost certainly know something you don't.

Losing it

In our early baking days, it's more than likely we will be 'ahead' of our dough, so the criteria used here to make judgement calls are focussed on things from this perspective.

That's because when we start out, we are keenly observing every little thing, so it tends to be a time where we 'wait' for things to happen.

Down the track, though, our perspective changes. Once we get better at making dough – whether this is from learning how to get better development by pre fermentation or by kneading, or by just 'reading' things better – the dough tends to rise more. When this happens, we will need to consider some new criteria, to do with avoiding over ripeness. Instead of 'waiting' for things to happen, we find ourselves running 'behind' the dough as it rises and ripens.

Overripe dough

A dough can become over ripe very quickly if it 'stews' in the tub. This happens when the dough runs out of air space above it to grow while it is still developing gas.

When the dough occupies the entire container, the container becomes a kind of pressure cooker. The temperature in the tub will rise – even if it is in the fridge at the time.

When the temperature rises, so too does the acidity level in the dough. When this occurs, our dough begins to 'break down'. This term refers to the gradual breaking down of the gluten bubbles. Yes, these are the same gluten bubbles we have spent careful time and attention in creating.

Once your dough begins to break down, there is no going back. There is no cure.
The best you can do for your dough when this happens is to get it into the oven as soon as you can. There is a chance you will get something edible from it – though don't expect a light or open crumb from this bread!

I keep a few old bread tins lying around for this purpose. Putting overripe dough in a bread tin will at least allow you to bake your dough, and if it hasn't broken down too much, the bread can be baked and eaten. It's very hard to sole bake overripe dough.

Dough that is overripe is really sticky. It tends to come away with your hand when touched. The surface of the dough could be termed as 'porous' – that is, it is 'pock marked', and there are holes present which seem to be there no matter which way the dough is turned.

Over ripeness can also occur if you haven't been keeping an eye on the temperature when making the dough.

Once a dough gets above about 25 degrees C in temperature, it is stepping outside the fermentation comfort zone.

Sourdough culture tends to do better in lower temperatures.

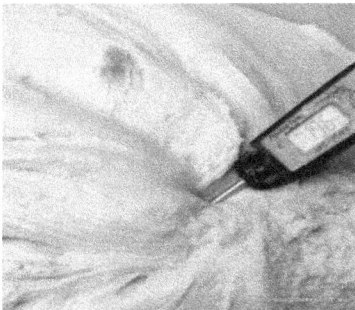

Cooler dough temperatures can definitely improve the fermentation process. And yes, this includes refrigeration. Particularly in hotter weather.

An upcoming short guide, the '**Really Slow Sourdough Fermentation Guide**', will contain lots more information about how to work with cool and cold fermentation. In the meantime, I will refer you to my Sourdough 101 Notes for more info.

The Three Bakery Seasons

In any bakery, including yours at home, there are three 'seasons'. They are as follows:

1/. **Too Fast Season** – usually mid-summer, and also mid bake when you are baking a lot at once and the temperature in the bakery is steadily rising.

2/. **Too Slow Season** – usually mid-winter, and at the beginning of any baking session, when nothing is happening fermentation wise, because there's not much heat around.

3/. **Comfortable Season** – Autumn, spring, and any time there is a sustained, even temperature range over a period of a few weeks or more. This season can occur in mid-summer or mid-winter as well.

Once we get used to conditions, we adapt. Acclimatizing to changes in the weather takes time though.

We bakers become comfortable with consistent conditions above all else. We, like many people, generally don't thrive on change.
It's interesting to note that human beings, like sourdough yeasts, inhabit 23 degrees C most of the time. If our environments are even a couple of degrees colder or warmer, we will modify the ambient temperature to keep ourselves comfortable.

Our houses are heated, cooled or engineered for this constant. So ambient temperature at home isn't really much of a variable. As home bakers, our seasonal 'variables' are just flour and water. If we happen to have an outdoor bakery (like I do), we also have to deal with the ambient temperature – but mostly, we live around a narrow bandwidth of temperature fluctuation.

Water temperatures vary enormously. On a hot summer's day, water from a domestic tap may come out at 30 degrees C. Flour from the cupboard could be 25 degrees. So between two ingredients, we have an average temperature of 27.5 degrees C.

On the other hand, in winter the water temp may be as little as 15 degrees C. The flour might be 20 C. So the average temperature of the two ingredients would be 17.5 degrees C.

Ten degrees difference between summer and winter! Every year I get emails and phone calls telling me that despite doing everything exactly the same, things have mysteriously changed. These types of calls and emails typically happen after a pronounced and consistent change in the weather.

Like farmers, bakers are beholden to the elements. Even those of us who bake year round, every day or week; the seasons always change, and we must move out of our relative comfort zone a few times every year.

Ways to deal with the Seasons

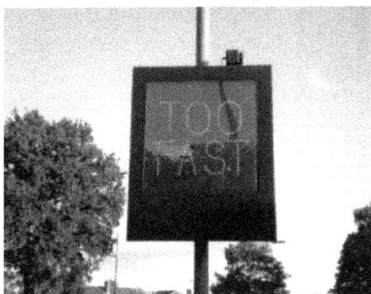

Too Fast Season:

During the summer months, everything is accelerated. Dough, no matter what stage it is going through in its process, ripens or gasses more quickly. It also seems to be larger.

Our strategy is to slow things down by reducing temperature. A few things we can do include:

- Make preferment a full 24 hours in advance, and leave it in the fridge so that it's fully cold when it comes time to make the dough from it.
- Store flour (and water if it is to be added when making the dough) in the fridge.
- Monitor dough temperatures through the proofing process, and take action as required For example, put dough in the fridge if it is above 25C.

Sometimes, warm dough is hard to handle – particularly when you are rough rounding or moulding into a cylinder. If this is the case, simply put the fully ripened dough in the fridge for an hour or two. This will make the dough firmer and therefore easier to round or mould. Protect dough from crusting up while it is proofing. On the final proof, things will really move along quickly. Make sure to preheat the oven well, so that it is ready to receive rapidly ripening dough.

Too Slow Season:

In midwinter, and through cold snaps, fermentation slows down. Ripening times are longer, and dough appears to be smaller, as less gas is being produced. A few things to consider include:

- Make your preferment with warm water – quite warm – and leave it out of the fridge for a few hours to begin fermentation.

- In really cold weather, you won't need to put it in the fridge at all.
- Find warm places – a window sill, above the coffee machine and so on – where dough can be ripened up.
- Warm up the room you are using. Running a woodfired oven will do that nicely.

Despite our best efforts, things will still happen slowly. Embrace the extra time. Relax, and allow things to happen without watching the clock. Go and do something ingenious while you are filling in time.

Comfortable Season:

The more regularly you make bread, the more you will become a creature of habit. Comfortable season is when your habits become vices. Once we become settled and our routine is set up around us, pretty soon the seasons will change and all those habits will prove to be, quite often, the thing that is holding us back from baking a decent loaf of bread.

How to deal with comfort season? Keep your eyes open. Keep records. Interrogate your method, by all means – but try to deal with one change at a time. There is a pretty decent chance that the issue, at any time, is to do with temperature management.

Make a mental note as you prepare your bake session to record the temperatures and times – particularly when you are starting out. I recommend a Baker's Diary to learn to read the seasons as well as dough. I still use this tool – and in my bakery, you will see blackboards full of production data.

It won't happen straight away, but over time you will begin to understand fermentation. When we make sourdough bread, we are dealing with a living process, a process which is used all around us, every day, in many different applications. Beer and wine, cheese, yogurt, sauerkraut, kimchi, kombucha, miso, soy sauce, sour cream – these things have all undergone a fermentation process of some kind.

Fermenting dough is very similar to fermenting many other things. Where bread is in a class of its own, though, is in the baking.
Our fermentation success (or otherwise) is captured by the oven at its optimal point. We get it right, and we feel immortal. We get it wrong, and life takes on a decidedly grey tone – for the baker, and for their customers, eager for delicious, fresh bread.

Baking is about the seasons, about timing, about history, politics and chemistry; it's about biology, engineering, farming and physics. And it's about satisfying a primal urge, deep within every one of us, to create something which nourishes us on a number of levels.

> *Sourdough fermentation is a great way to make nutritious bread at home without using refined yeast or bread improvers of any kind.*

Conclusion

It is the original bread, having been made by humans for thousands of years. Its rediscovery in recent times reminds us of just how far we have come from our prehistoric roots. At the same time, in our never ending quest for progress, we seem to have lost the connection we had to this primal and deeply satisfying process of self nutrition.

This series of mini guides will cover various aspects of this very old and very challenging craft. Keep an eye out for these and other upcoming guides:

The Really Slow Sourdough Fermentation Guide

The Definitive Guide to Sole Baking

The White Oven Project

Better Dough Development

Ancient Grains for Modern Bread

The Really Good Guide to Bread Ovens

www.ingramcontent.com/pod-product-compliance
Lightning Source LLC
Chambersburg PA
CBHW020440030426
42337CB00014B/1331